*You are capable, you are deserving,
and you have the power to detach and embrace a life
of authenticity and joy.*

introduction

This book has been written with the intention of providing guidance and support to those who are seeking to detach from a person who no longer serves their well-being. We understand that detachment is a complex and deeply personal process, and our aim is to empower you with practical tools and insights to navigate this transformative journey with grace and resilience.

You are not alone in this journey. Many have walked this path before you, and their stories and experiences have contributed to the wisdom and insights shared within these pages. It is our hope that through this guide, you will find solace, inspiration, and the tools needed to embark on a transformative journey of detachment, ultimately rediscovering the essence of who you truly are.

May this guide be a guiding light on your path to detachment and self-empowerment, helping you reclaim your autonomy, heal your heart, and embrace a future filled with possibilities.

Welcome to "How do I Detach from Someone? A Guide to Detaching and Rediscovering Yourself." Let the journey begin.

Emotional Awareness & Healing

Emotional Awareness and Healing is essential for detaching from unhealthy relationships and rediscovering oneself. It encourages individuals to reflect on their emotions, learn from past experiences, and foster self-compassion throughout the detachment process.

I

acknowledge your emotions

Recognize and accept your feelings about the situation. It's normal to feel sadness, anger, or confusion when detaching from someone.

Emotions play a significant role in the process of detaching from someone. Acknowledging and accepting your feelings is an essential step towards healing and moving forward. It is normal to experience a range of emotions, such as sadness, anger, and confusion, as you detach from someone who has been a significant part of your life. By allowing yourself to recognize and accept these emotions, you create space for self-reflection, healing, and personal growth.

Practicing acknowledgment of your emotions involves creating a safe and non-judgmental space for yourself to explore and experience them. It is essential to be gentle and compassionate with yourself during this process. Allow yourself to fully feel and express your emotions without suppressing or invalidating them. Embrace the understanding that your feelings are valid and that it is okay to experience a mix of emotions as you navigate the detachment process.

Examples of how to practice acknowledging your emotions:
- Create a quiet and comfortable space for self-reflection and emotional exploration.
- Engage in journaling to express and process your emotions.
- Seek support from a therapist or counselor to guide you in recognizing and accepting your feelings.
- Practice mindfulness or meditation to observe and acknowledge your emotions without judgment.
- Talk to trusted friends or family members who can provide a listening ear and understanding.

II
practice emotional release techniques

Explore practices such as deep breathing, meditation, or mindfulness exercises to release emotional tension and promote inner calmness.

Emotional release techniques are powerful tools that can help you let go of emotional tension and find inner calmness on your journey of detachment and personal growth. This chapter delves into the importance of practicing emotional release techniques and provides guidance on incorporating them into your daily life.

Engaging in practices such as deep breathing, meditation, or mindfulness exercises allows you to connect with your emotions and release any accumulated tension within your body and mind. These techniques help you cultivate a sense of inner calmness and create space for healing and growth. By acknowledging and releasing your emotions, you pave the way for greater emotional well-being and a healthier relationship with yourself and others.

Here are some examples of how to practice emotional release techniques:
- Deep breathing exercises: Take slow, deep breaths, inhaling through your nose and exhaling through your mouth. Focus on the sensation of your breath filling your lungs and gradually release any tension with each exhale.
- Meditation: Find a quiet and comfortable space where you can sit in a relaxed position. Close your eyes and bring your attention to your breath or a specific point of focus, allowing thoughts and emotions to come and go without judgment.
- Mindfulness exercises: Engage in activities such as mindful walking, body scans, or mindful eating. Pay attention to the present moment, fully experiencing the sensations, thoughts, and emotions that arise without attachment or judgment.

III
practice acceptance and self-forgiveness

Accept the past, forgive yourself for any perceived mistakes or shortcomings, and let go of self-blame. Embracing acceptance and self-forgiveness is crucial for moving forward and cultivating inner peace.

In the process of detachment and personal growth, practicing acceptance and self-forgiveness plays a vital role. It involves acknowledging the past, accepting the realities of your experiences, and releasing any self-blame or guilt that may be holding you back. By embracing acceptance and self-forgiveness, you create space for healing, compassion, and inner peace. In this chapter, we will explore the importance of practicing acceptance and self-forgiveness and provide guidance on how to incorporate them into your life.

Acceptance is about acknowledging the past without resistance or judgment. It's an act of surrendering to what has happened and recognizing that you cannot change it. Acceptance allows you to let go of the need to control or hold onto what is no longer serving you. By accepting the past, you open yourself up to the present moment and create room for growth and new possibilities.

Self-forgiveness is an essential aspect of the detachment process. It involves letting go of self-blame, guilt, and harsh judgments toward yourself. Recognize that everyone makes mistakes and that you are deserving of forgiveness, including from yourself. Self-forgiveness is a powerful act of compassion and self-love that allows you to release the weight of the past and move forward with a lighter heart.

Here are some examples of how to practice acceptance & self-forgiveness:
- Journaling: Write about your experiences, emotions, and thoughts. Use this as an opportunity to reflect, gain clarity, and cultivate self-compassion.
- Mindfulness and meditation: Practice mindfulness to bring awareness to the present moment and observe your thoughts and emotions without judgment. Engage in self-forgiveness meditations to consciously release self-blame and cultivate self-compassion.
- Seek support: Consider seeking the guidance of a therapist, counselor, or support group. They can provide a safe space for you to explore your feelings, gain insights, and receive support on your journey toward acceptance and self-forgiveness.

IV

practice acceptance

Recognize that detachment is a process that involves accepting the reality of the situation. Allow yourself to accept the past, the present, and the uncertainties of the future. Embracing acceptance can help you find peace and move forward.

Detachment is a transformative journey that requires embracing acceptance as a fundamental practice. It involves acknowledging and embracing the reality of the situation, including the past, the present, and the uncertainties of the future. By practicing acceptance, you release resistance and create space for inner peace, healing, and growth.

Acceptance does not mean condoning or approving of what has transpired; rather, it is an active choice to let go of the need for control and surrender to what is. It involves acknowledging the impermanence of relationships and the unpredictable nature of life. When you practice acceptance, you cultivate resilience, mindfulness, and an ability to navigate the detachment process with grace and wisdom.

Examples of how to practice acceptance:
- Engage in mindfulness meditation to cultivate a non-judgmental awareness of the present moment and accept things as they are.
- Practice self-compassion by offering kindness and understanding to yourself as you navigate the complexities of detachment.
- Seek support from others who have experienced similar situations, joining support groups or seeking guidance from a therapist.
- Embrace uncertainty and learn to be comfortable with the unknown, trusting in the process of life and your own resilience.
- Cultivate gratitude for the lessons learned, the growth experienced, and the opportunities for self-discovery that detachment brings.

V

reflect on lessons learned

Take time to reflect on the lessons and insights gained from the relationship. Identify the ways in which it has contributed to your personal growth and self-awareness.

In the process of detachment, taking the time to reflect on the lessons learned from the relationship can be a valuable step towards personal growth and self-awareness. Reflecting on the experiences and insights gained can provide clarity, closure, and a deeper understanding of oneself. This chapter explores the importance of reflection and offers guidance on how to engage in this introspective practice.

Reflection allows you to gain a new perspective on the relationship and its impact on your life. It offers an opportunity to uncover valuable lessons that can shape your future decisions and relationships.

Here are some ways to practice reflection and embrace personal growth:
- Journaling: Set aside dedicated time to write in a journal and express your thoughts, emotions, and reflections on the relationship. Consider the following prompts:
    - What were the key lessons I learned from this relationship?
    - How did this relationship contribute to my personal growth?
    - What patterns or behaviors do I want to change moving forward?
    - What strengths or qualities did I discover about myself through this experience?
- Seeking Support: Engage in conversations with trusted friends, family members, or a therapist who can provide a supportive and non-judgmental space for you to reflect on the relationship. Talking through your experiences can offer new insights and perspectives.
- Self-Reflection Practices: Incorporate self-reflection practices into your routine, such as meditation, mindfulness exercises, or engaging in activities that promote introspection and self-awareness. This can help you gain clarity and deepen your understanding of yourself and your experiences.

VI

reflect on your values and priorities

Take time to reassess your values and priorities in life. Detaching from someone can create space for self-reflection and allow you to align your choices and actions with what truly matters to you.

Detaching from someone presents an opportunity for deep self-reflection and introspection. It allows you to reevaluate your values and priorities, ensuring that your choices and actions align with what truly matters to you. By taking the time to reflect on your values and priorities, you can make conscious decisions that lead to a more authentic and fulfilling life.

Reflecting on your values involves identifying the principles and beliefs that guide your life. Consider what is truly important to you, what brings you meaning and fulfillment, and what you aspire to embody. Reassessing your priorities involves determining how you want to allocate your time, energy, and resources in alignment with your values.

Examples of how to reflect on your values and priorities:
- Engage in solitude and create a space for introspection, allowing your thoughts and emotions to surface.
- Journal about your core values, exploring how they shape your decisions and actions.
- Seek inspiration from role models or individuals who embody the values and priorities you aspire to have.
- Consider your long-term goals and evaluate if they align with your values and priorities.
- Engage in conversations with trusted friends or mentors who can provide different perspectives and insights.

VII

cultivate mindfulness in everyday life

Bring mindfulness into your daily routines. Pay attention to your thoughts, feelings, and sensations in the present moment without judgment. This can help you detach from past attachments and cultivate inner peace.

Mindfulness is a practice that invites us to fully engage with the present moment, free from judgment or attachment. When we cultivate mindfulness in our everyday lives, we develop a deeper awareness of our thoughts, feelings, and sensations. This chapter explores how incorporating mindfulness into your daily routines can support the process of detachment and foster inner peace.

Mindfulness can be practiced in various ways throughout your day. Whether it's during mundane activities like washing dishes or more intentional practices such as meditation, the goal is to bring your attention to the present moment. By doing so, you create space to observe your thoughts and emotions without becoming entangled in them. This awareness helps you detach from past attachments and prevents your mind from dwelling on the past or worrying about the future.

Here are some examples of how to cultivate mindfulness in everyday life:
- Start your day with a few moments of mindful breathing or a short meditation to set a positive tone for the day.
- Engage in everyday activities with full presence and attention. Notice the sensations, sounds, and sights around you as you perform tasks like eating, walking, or taking a shower.
- Take regular mindfulness breaks throughout the day. Pause for a few moments to close your eyes, take a few deep breaths, and check in with yourself.

VIII

challenge negative thoughts

Detachment can sometimes bring up negative thoughts and self-doubt. Practice challenging and reframing those thoughts with more positive and empowering ones. Focus on your strengths and the progress you've made.

During the process of detachment, negative thoughts and self-doubt may arise, clouding your perception and hindering your progress. It's essential to practice challenging and reframing those thoughts, replacing them with more positive and empowering perspectives. By consciously shifting your mindset, you can cultivate a supportive inner dialogue and strengthen your belief in yourself.

Challenging negative thoughts involves becoming aware of your self-talk and questioning the validity of the thoughts that arise. Recognize that negative thoughts are often distorted and not reflective of reality. Instead of accepting them at face value, actively challenge their accuracy and reframe them in a more empowering and realistic light. Focus on your strengths, resilience, and the progress you've made in your detachment journey.

Examples of how to challenge negative thoughts:
- Practice mindfulness to observe your thoughts without judgment, allowing you to recognize negative patterns and interrupt them.
- Keep a thought journal to record negative thoughts and challenge them by providing evidence against their validity.
- Seek support from friends, family, or a therapist who can provide objective perspectives and help you reframe negative thoughts.
- Engage in positive affirmations, repeating empowering statements that counteract negative self-talk.
- Surround yourself with positive influences, whether through uplifting books, podcasts, or communities that foster a positive mindset.

IX

practice gratitude journaling

Write down three things you are grateful for each day. This practice can help shift your focus towards the positive aspects of your life and cultivate a sense of appreciation and contentment.

Gratitude journaling is a powerful tool for fostering a positive mindset and enhancing your overall well-being. This chapter delves into the practice of gratitude journaling and its benefits in the process of detachment. By consciously acknowledging and appreciating the blessings in your life, you can shift your perspective and cultivate a sense of gratitude and contentment.

Gratitude journaling involves the simple act of writing down three things you are grateful for each day. It can be as specific or as general as you like, focusing on big or small moments, people, experiences, or things. The key is to bring your attention to the positive aspects of your life and to develop a habit of recognizing and appreciating them.

Here are some examples of how to practice gratitude journaling:
- Set aside a few minutes each day to reflect on your day and identify three things you are grateful for. Write them down in a dedicated gratitude journal or notebook.
- Be specific and descriptive. Instead of simply listing broad categories like "family" or "health," delve deeper and specify the reasons or aspects of those relationships or your well-being that you are grateful for.
- Embrace the present moment. Focus on what is happening in your life right now and find gratitude in the small joys and simple pleasures that surround you.

Self-Care & Personal Growth

Self-Care and Personal Growth encourages individuals to invest time and energy in themselves, acknowledging that their needs and desires are essential for a balanced and fulfilling life.

X

focus on self-care

Take care of yourself physically, emotionally, and mentally. Engage in activities that bring you joy, such as hobbies, exercise, spending time with loved ones, or practicing mindfulness and self-reflection.

During the process of detaching from someone, it is crucial to prioritize self-care. Taking care of yourself physically, emotionally, and mentally plays a significant role in healing and moving forward. By engaging in activities that bring you joy, practicing self-reflection, and surrounding yourself with supportive loved ones, you create a foundation for self-nurturing and personal growth.

Self-care encompasses various aspects of your well-being. Physically, it involves nourishing your body with nutritious food, getting enough restful sleep, and engaging in regular exercise. Emotionally, it involves acknowledging and expressing your feelings, seeking support from trusted individuals, and engaging in activities that bring you joy and peace. Mentally, it involves practicing mindfulness and self-reflection, engaging in hobbies and interests, and cultivating positive self-talk and self-compassion.

Examples of how to practice self-care:
- Engage in regular physical exercise that suits your interests and abilities, such as yoga, swimming, or walking.
- Allocate time for activities that bring you joy and relaxation, such as reading, listening to music, or spending time in nature.
- Seek support from loved ones or a support group who can provide a listening ear and understanding.
- Practice mindfulness and self-reflection through meditation, journaling, or deep breathing exercises.
- Set aside time for self-reflection and self-discovery to gain insight into your needs, desires, and aspirations.
- Prioritize restful sleep by establishing a consistent bedtime routine and creating a comfortable sleep environment.

XI

create a self-care routine

Develop a regular self-care routine that encompasses activities that nourish your physical, emotional, and mental well-being. This could include activities such as meditation, taking baths, practicing self-care rituals, or engaging in hobbies that bring you joy.

In the midst of life's demands and responsibilities, it is crucial to prioritize self-care as an integral part of your well-being. Creating a self-care routine allows you to nurture and replenish yourself physically, emotionally, and mentally. This chapter explores the importance of self-care and provides guidance on how to develop a personalized self-care routine that supports your overall well-being.

Self-care encompasses a range of activities that promote self-nurturing and holistic well-being. It is a conscious and intentional practice that allows you to take care of your physical, emotional, and mental health. By incorporating self-care into your daily life, you can recharge, reduce stress, and cultivate a greater sense of balance and happiness.

Here are some examples of how to practice & create a self-care routine:
- Identify your self-care needs: Reflect on the activities or practices that help you feel relaxed, rejuvenated, and fulfilled. Consider what brings you joy, peace, and a sense of well-being.
- Prioritize self-care activities: Make self-care a priority by scheduling dedicated time for self-care activities in your daily or weekly routine. Treat this time as non-negotiable and essential for your well-being.
- Engage in a variety of self-care activities: Explore different self-care practices and find a balance that works for you. This may include physical activities like exercise or yoga, engaging in hobbies or creative outlets, practicing mindfulness or meditation, or enjoying moments of solitude and relaxation.
- Practice self-compassion: Be gentle and kind to yourself throughout your self-care journey. Understand that self-care is not selfish but essential for your overall well-being. Release any guilt or judgment associated with taking time for yourself.
- Adapt and adjust as needed: Your self-care routine may evolve over time, and that's okay. Listen to your needs and adjust your self-care activities as necessary. Be open to trying new practices and finding what truly nourishes you.

XII

set boundaries with yourself

Establish personal boundaries that honor your needs, desires, and well-being. This includes saying no to activities or situations that do not align with your values or deplete your energy.

Setting boundaries is a vital aspect of self-care and personal growth. In this chapter, we explore the importance of establishing boundaries with yourself and provide guidance on how to practice this essential skill for your overall well-being.

Creating personal boundaries involves identifying and honoring your needs, desires, and values. It means recognizing when to say no to activities or situations that do not serve you or align with your priorities. By setting boundaries with yourself, you create a foundation of self-respect and self-care, allowing you to prioritize your well-being and cultivate a healthier relationship with yourself.

Here are some examples of how to practice setting boundaries with yourself:
- Reflect on your needs: Take time to reflect on what you truly need in various areas of your life, such as relationships, work, and personal time. Identify your limits and what is important to you.
- Establish clear boundaries: Communicate your boundaries to yourself by setting clear limits on your time, energy, and resources. Define what is acceptable and what is not in terms of how you treat yourself and allow others to treat you.
- Practice self-compassion: Be kind and compassionate with yourself as you navigate setting boundaries. Understand that it is a process, and it is okay to make adjustments along the way. Treat yourself with the same respect and care that you would offer to others.

XIII

establish new routines and habits

Introduce new routines and habits into your daily life. This helps create a sense of structure and stability, facilitating the detachment process and allowing space for personal growth.

Establishing new routines and habits is a powerful way to support your detachment process and promote personal growth. By consciously introducing structure into your daily life, you create a sense of stability and purpose, providing a solid foundation for your journey of detachment and self-discovery. In this chapter, we will explore the importance of establishing new routines and habits and discover practical ways to incorporate them into your life.

New routines and habits can help break free from old patterns and create a fresh start. They provide a framework for healthy and productive behaviors, allowing you to focus on your personal growth and well-being. Whether it's establishing a morning routine, implementing regular exercise, or incorporating mindful practices into your day, new routines and habits can contribute to your overall sense of balance, clarity, and fulfillment.

Here are some examples of how to practice establishing new routines and habits:

- Morning routine: Start your day with a consistent morning routine that sets a positive tone for the rest of the day. This can include activities such as meditation, journaling, exercise, or reading.
- Exercise routine: Dedicate specific times in your week to engage in physical activities that you enjoy. Whether it's going for a jog, attending a yoga class, or participating in a team sport, regular exercise can boost your energy levels, improve your mood, and enhance your overall well-being.
- Self-care habits: Incorporate self-care practices into your daily life to nurture your mind, body, and soul. This can involve activities such as taking relaxing baths, practicing mindfulness or meditation, engaging in creative pursuits, or spending time in nature.

XIV

focus on personal goals

Set and pursue personal goals that align with your values and aspirations. Directing your energy towards your own growth and achievements can help shift the focus away from the person you're detaching from.

In the process of detachment, focusing on personal goals becomes a powerful catalyst for self-discovery, growth, and redirection of energy. By setting and pursuing goals that are meaningful and aligned with our values and aspirations, we shift our attention away from the person we are detaching from and channel it towards our own journey of self-improvement. Personal goals provide a sense of purpose, motivation, and a roadmap to navigate through challenges and embrace new opportunities.

Setting personal goals involves identifying what truly matters to us and envisioning the kind of life we want to create. It requires introspection, self-awareness, and a deep understanding of our values, passions, and aspirations. By clarifying our goals, we can create a sense of direction and focus, guiding our actions and decisions towards personal fulfillment and growth.

Examples of focusing on personal goals:
- Identify specific and measurable goals that reflect your passions, interests, and values.
- Break down larger goals into smaller, actionable steps to make them more manageable and achievable.
- Create a timeline or schedule to track your progress and hold yourself accountable.
- Seek support and guidance from mentors, coaches, or friends who can provide guidance and encouragement along your journey.
- Celebrate milestones and achievements as you make progress towards your goals, reinforcing a sense of accomplishment and motivation.

XV

establish a healthy routine

Create a structured and balanced daily routine that incorporates activities that promote your well-being. This can provide a sense of stability and purpose as you navigate the detachment process.

A healthy routine encompasses a variety of activities that contribute to your overall well-being, including physical, mental, and emotional aspects. By intentionally incorporating these activities into your daily schedule, you create a framework that supports your detachment process and promotes personal growth.

Here are some key elements to consider when establishing a healthy routine:

- Self-Care Practices: Allocate time for self-care activities that nourish your mind, body, and spirit. This can include practices such as:
  - Meditation or mindfulness exercises
  - Journaling or reflective writing
  - Engaging in hobbies or creative pursuits
  - Spending time in nature or practicing outdoor activities
- Balanced Nutrition: Prioritize healthy eating habits by including a variety of nutrient-rich foods in your meals. Aim for a balanced diet that consists of:
  - Fruits and vegetables
  - Whole grains
  - Lean proteins
  - Healthy fats
  - Drinking an adequate amount of water throughout the day
- Regular Sleep Schedule: Establish a consistent sleep routine to ensure you get sufficient rest. Consider the following:
  - Set a regular bedtime and wake-up time
  - Create a relaxing evening routine
  - Avoid electronic devices before bed

XVI

practice self-empowering activities

Focus on activities that promote self-growth and empowerment. This can include taking up a new hobby, learning new skills, or setting personal goals to boost your self-esteem and confidence.

Engaging in self-empowering activities is a powerful way to detach from someone and foster personal growth. By focusing on activities that promote self-improvement, you can enhance your self-esteem, boost your confidence, and cultivate a strong sense of empowerment. This can involve exploring new hobbies, acquiring new skills, or setting personal goals that align with your passions and aspirations.

Consider the activities that ignite your curiosity and bring you joy. Is there a hobby you've always wanted to try? A skill you've been interested in learning? Now is the perfect time to embark on these endeavors. By engaging in self-empowering activities, you invest in your personal development and create a sense of fulfillment and accomplishment independent of the previous relationship.

Examples of how to practice engaging in self-empowering activities:
- Explore a new hobby or revisit an old one that brings you joy and fulfillment.
- Enroll in a class or workshop to learn a new skill or develop existing talents.
- Set personal goals that align with your passions and aspirations, and work towards achieving them.
- Engage in activities that promote self-care and self-reflection, such as meditation, journaling, or practicing mindfulness.
- Surround yourself with supportive and like-minded individuals who encourage and inspire your personal growth.
- Celebrate your achievements, no matter how small, and acknowledge your progress along the way.

XVII

rediscover your passions

Reconnect with the things that bring you joy and passion. Engage in activities or hobbies that you may have neglected during the relationship or discover new ones that ignite your enthusiasm.

Reconnecting with your passions is an essential part of the journey towards personal growth and self-fulfillment. When detaching from someone, it is common to lose sight of your own interests and hobbies. However, by rediscovering your passions, you can reignite your sense of self and tap into a source of joy and fulfillment. This chapter will guide you on the path to rediscovering your passions and embracing them as an integral part of your life.

One way to practice rediscovering your passions is by reflecting on your past interests and activities that brought you joy. Think about the things you used to love doing before the relationship took center stage in your life. Additionally, be open to exploring new hobbies or activities that pique your curiosity.

Here are some examples of how to practice rediscovering your passions:

- Make a list of activities you used to enjoy and prioritize incorporating them back into your routine.
- Explore new hobbies or interests that you have always wanted to try.
- Join clubs or groups centered around your passions to connect with like-minded individuals.
- Create a vision board that represents your interests and goals, helping you stay focused on your passions.

XVIII

engage in creative outlets

Explore your creativity through activities such as painting, writing, music, or crafts. Expressing yourself creatively can help process emotions and provide a sense of release.

Engaging in creative outlets is a powerful way to navigate the process of detachment. Creativity offers a channel for expressing your emotions, thoughts, and experiences in a unique and personal way. Whether it's through painting, writing, music, or crafts, embracing your creative side can provide a sense of release, healing, and self-discovery. By allowing yourself to explore different artistic mediums, you open the door to new forms of expression and find solace in the creative process.

Creativity serves as a bridge between your inner world and the external reality. It allows you to tap into your emotions and experiences, giving them shape and form through your chosen artistic outlet. This act of creation helps you process and make sense of the complexities of detachment, enabling you to explore your emotions and find a sense of catharsis. It also offers a means of communication and connection, as your creative expressions can resonate with others who have shared similar experiences.

Examples of how to practice engaging in creative outlets:
- Set aside dedicated time each day or week to engage in your chosen creative activity.
- Experiment with different artistic mediums to find the one that resonates with you the most.
- Allow yourself to create without judgment or pressure, embracing the process rather than focusing solely on the outcome.
- Use your creative outlet as a means of self-reflection and exploration, allowing your emotions and thoughts to guide your artistic expression.
- Consider joining a creative group or workshop where you can share your work, receive feedback, and connect with like-minded individuals.

XIX

set new goals

Set meaningful goals for yourself that are independent of the person you're detaching from. This can help you shift your focus and create a sense of purpose and fulfillment in your life.

The journey of detachment offers a unique opportunity for self-discovery and personal growth. As you detach from someone, you create space to explore your own desires, values, and aspirations. Embracing self-discovery allows you to uncover your true potential and pave the way for a more fulfilling and authentic life.

During this process, take time to reflect on your own needs, passions, and dreams. Explore different aspects of yourself and engage in activities that align with your values and bring you joy. Embrace curiosity and a sense of adventure as you embark on this voyage of self-discovery.

Examples of how to embrace self-discovery:
- Engage in self-reflection through journaling, introspection, or therapy to uncover your authentic self and gain clarity on your values and aspirations.
- Try new experiences and step outside your comfort zone to discover new passions and interests.
- Surround yourself with supportive and like-minded individuals who encourage your self-discovery journey.
- Set personal goals and work towards them, allowing yourself to grow and evolve in the process.
- Practice self-care rituals that nourish your mind, body, and soul, fostering a deeper connection with yourself.

XX

engage in physical activities

Participate in physical activities that promote the release of endorphins and boost your overall well-being. Exercise, dance, or engage in sports to help reduce stress and improve your mood.

Engaging in physical activities is a powerful way to support your detachment process and promote overall well-being. This chapter explores the importance of incorporating physical activities into your routine and how they can help release endorphins, reduce stress, and improve your mood. By prioritizing your physical health, you can enhance your emotional resilience and create a positive impact on your detachment journey.

Physical activities such as exercise, dance, or sports offer numerous benefits for your mental and emotional well-being. They stimulate the release of endorphins, which are natural mood-enhancing chemicals in the brain. These endorphins help reduce stress, improve sleep quality, and increase feelings of happiness and well-being. Engaging in physical activities also provides a healthy outlet to release tension and pent-up emotions, allowing you to clear your mind and improve your overall emotional state.

Here are some examples of how to practice engaging in physical activities:
- Incorporate regular exercise into your routine, such as walking, jogging, cycling, or attending fitness classes. Aim for at least 30 minutes of moderate-intensity exercise most days of the week.
- Explore activities that bring you joy and excitement, such as dancing, swimming, hiking, or playing a favorite sport. Find activities that resonate with you and make you feel energized and alive.
- Create a balanced exercise routine that includes a mix of cardiovascular activities, strength training, and flexibility exercises. This will help you improve your overall fitness and promote a holistic approach to physical well-being.

XXI

create a vision board

Visualize your desired future and create a vision board that represents the life you want to build for yourself. Include images, quotes, and symbols that inspire and motivate you to move forward.

Creating a vision board is a powerful tool for manifesting your desired future and providing visual inspiration on your detachment journey. This chapter explores the significance of vision boards and how they can help you clarify your goals, stay focused, and maintain motivation. By engaging in this creative process, you can bring your dreams to life and set a clear direction for the future you envision.

A vision board is a collage of images, quotes, and symbols that represent your goals, aspirations, and desires. It serves as a visual representation of the life you want to create for yourself. By regularly observing your vision board, you reinforce positive thoughts and emotions associated with your goals, and you begin to align your actions and choices with your vision. This process helps keep you motivated, inspired, and focused on your journey of detachment and personal growth.

Here are some examples of how to practice creating a vision board:
- Gather magazines, printed images, quotes, or symbols that resonate with your aspirations and values. Choose materials that evoke positive emotions and reflect the future you want to create.
- Set aside dedicated time and find a quiet, comfortable space to work on your vision board. Allow yourself to be fully present in the process and let your creativity flow.
- Arrange the images, quotes, and symbols on a poster board or any other surface that feels right for you. Use glue, tape, or other adhesive methods to secure the items in place.
- Display your vision board in a prominent location where you can see it daily. Take a few moments each day to observe your vision board, visualize your desired future, and connect with the feelings and emotions associated with your goals.

XXII

cultivate new connections

Invest time in building new relationships and nurturing existing ones. Surround yourself with people who uplift and support you, as they can help fill the void left by detaching from the person.

As you detach from someone, it is essential to invest time and energy in cultivating new connections. Building new relationships and nurturing existing ones can provide a sense of support, belonging, and fulfillment. Surrounding yourself with people who uplift and support you can help fill the void left by detaching from the person and contribute to your overall well-being and growth.

Look for opportunities to meet new people who share your interests and values. Join social or community groups, attend events or workshops, or explore online communities centered around your hobbies or passions. Actively engage in conversations and activities that foster connection and allow you to forge meaningful relationships. Additionally, don't overlook the importance of nurturing existing relationships with friends and family. Invest time in strengthening these bonds, as they can offer valuable support and understanding during the detachment process.

Examples of how to practice cultivating new connections:
- Attend social events, meetups, or networking gatherings related to your interests or professional field.
- Join clubs, organizations, or hobby groups that align with your passions.
- Volunteer for a cause that resonates with you, connecting with like-minded individuals who share your values.
- Take part in online communities or forums centered around your hobbies or areas of interest.
- Initiate social outings with friends or family, creating opportunities for quality time and meaningful conversations.
- Practice active listening and empathy when engaging with others, fostering deeper connections and understanding.

XXIII

surround yourself with positive influences

Seek out individuals who inspire and uplift you. Surrounding yourself with positive, supportive people can foster a sense of community and encourage personal growth.

Surrounding yourself with positive influences is a powerful step in the detachment process. This chapter explores the importance of seeking out individuals who inspire and uplift you, as well as the impact they can have on your personal growth and well-being. By consciously surrounding yourself with positive and supportive people, you create a community that fosters positivity, encouragement, and personal development.

Positive influences can come in various forms, including friends, family members, mentors, colleagues, or even virtual communities. These individuals radiate positivity, offer support, and inspire you to become the best version of yourself. By surrounding yourself with such influences, you create an environment that uplifts and motivates you throughout the detachment journey.

Here are some examples of how to practice surrounding yourself with positive influences:
- Cultivate supportive relationships: Seek out individuals who genuinely care about your well-being and encourage your personal growth. Surround yourself with people who provide emotional support, offer constructive feedback, and believe in your potential.
- Engage in positive communities: Join groups or communities that align with your interests, values, or goals. These communities can be in-person or online, and they can provide a space for shared experiences, inspiration, and mutual support.
- Limit exposure to negativity: Evaluate your social media feeds, news consumption, and other sources of information. Minimize exposure to negativity and focus on content that uplifts and inspires you. Unfollow accounts or unsubscribe from sources that consistently bring you down.

XXIV

volunteer to help others

Channel your energy into making a positive impact in the lives of others. Volunteering or engaging in acts of kindness can shift your focus outward and bring a sense of fulfillment and purpose.

One of the most powerful ways to heal and find fulfillment during the detachment process is to extend a helping hand to others. When you shift your focus from your own pain to making a positive impact in the lives of others, you not only contribute to their well-being but also experience a profound sense of fulfillment and purpose. This chapter will explore the importance of volunteering and helping others as a means to heal and grow.

Volunteering offers a unique opportunity to connect with your community and make a meaningful difference. It allows you to use your skills, talents, and time to support causes that resonate with you. By giving back, you gain a sense of purpose and connection to something larger than yourself.

Here are some examples of how to practice volunteering or helping others:
- Research local nonprofits or organizations that align with your values and interests.
- Offer your time and skills to support community initiatives, such as mentoring, tutoring, or assisting in fundraising events.
- Volunteer at a shelter, hospital, or community center to provide assistance to those in need.
- Engage in random acts of kindness, such as buying a meal for someone in need or helping a neighbor with their chores.

XXV

practice self soothing activities

Identify activities that bring you comfort and peace, such as taking a warm bath, listening to calming music, practicing aromatherapy, or engaging in relaxation techniques like deep breathing or progressive muscle relaxation.

It is essential to prioritize self-care and engage in activities that bring comfort and peace to our lives. These self-soothing practices can provide a much-needed respite from the challenges of detaching and foster a sense of calm and well-being. By identifying and incorporating these activities into our daily routines, we can create a nurturing environment that supports our emotional healing and growth.

Here are some examples of self-soothing activities that can be practiced:

- Taking a warm bath: Indulge in a relaxing bath with soothing bath salts or essential oils. Allow the warm water to envelop you and release any tension or stress.
- Listening to calming music: Create a playlist of gentle, soothing music or nature sounds that help you unwind and find inner peace. Find a comfortable spot to sit or lie down, close your eyes, and let the music wash over you.
- Practicing aromatherapy: Use essential oils with calming properties, such as lavender or chamomile, to create a serene atmosphere. Diffuse the oils in your living space or apply them topically to experience their soothing effects.
- Deep breathing: Practice deep breathing exercises to promote relaxation and reduce anxiety. Take slow, deep breaths, focusing on each inhale and exhale, allowing your body to relax with each breath.

Detachment & Mindset Shift

Detachment and Mindset Shift explores various techniques and practices that help individuals detach from negative emotions, limiting beliefs, and unhealthy patterns. It encourages letting go of expectations, accepting the present moment, and redirecting focus towards personal growth and self-empowerment.

XXVI

let go of expectations

Release any expectations you may have had about the person or the relationship. Understand that you cannot control or change others; you can only control your own actions and reactions.

Letting go of expectations is a powerful step in the process of detaching from someone. It involves releasing any preconceived notions or hopes you may have had about the person or the relationship. Recognize that you cannot control or change others; you can only control your own actions and reactions. By embracing acceptance and personal empowerment, you free yourself from the emotional burden of unfulfilled expectations and create space for personal growth and emotional well-being.

Releasing expectations requires a shift in perspective and a willingness to detach from outcomes. Understand that individuals have their own paths, choices, and limitations. Embrace the fact that you cannot force someone to change or meet your expectations. Instead, focus on accepting them as they are and directing your energy towards self-improvement and creating a fulfilling life for yourself.

Examples of how to practice letting go of expectations:
- Reflect on your expectations and identify the ones that are causing you emotional distress or disappointment.
- Challenge and reframe unrealistic or unhealthy expectations by focusing on acceptance and adaptability.
- Practice mindfulness and self-awareness to recognize when expectations arise and consciously choose to let them go.
- Cultivate gratitude for the positive aspects of the relationship or the lessons learned, rather than dwelling on unmet expectations.
- Redirect your focus and energy towards personal growth, hobbies, and interests that bring you fulfillment and joy.

XXVII

limit reminders

Minimize exposure to triggers or reminders of the person or the relationship. This may involve removing their photos or belongings from your living space or unfollowing them on social media.

Limiting reminders of the person or the relationship is an important step in the process of detaching. By minimizing exposure to triggers or reminders, you create a supportive environment for healing and moving forward. This may involve removing physical reminders, such as photos or belongings, from your living space, as well as taking steps to reduce their presence in your digital life, such as unfollowing or muting them on social media.

Reminders can evoke strong emotions and hinder the detachment process. They have the power to bring back memories and stir up feelings of longing, sadness, or nostalgia. By intentionally creating distance from these reminders, you allow yourself the space and freedom to heal and focus on your own well-being. It's important to remember that this is a personal choice and may vary depending on the individual and the specific circumstances of the relationship.

Examples of how to practice limiting reminders:
- Remove or store away physical reminders, such as gifts, letters, or photographs, that trigger strong emotions.
- Consider rearranging your living space to create a fresh and new environment that feels supportive and uplifting.
- Unfollow, mute, or hide the person's social media accounts to reduce exposure to their posts and updates.
- Take breaks from social media altogether to minimize the chances of stumbling upon reminders of the person.
- Surround yourself with new experiences, hobbies, or decor that symbolize new beginnings and reflect your own personal growth.
- Replace reminders of the person with items that bring you joy, peace, and inspiration.

XXVIII

redirect your focus

Find healthy distractions that redirect your focus away from the person you're detaching from. This could involve immersing yourself in engaging books, movies, hobbies, or activities that bring you joy.

Engaging in positive distractions can be a powerful tool to redirect your focus away from the person you're detaching from. These distractions provide a healthy and productive way to occupy your mind and emotions, allowing you to create space for healing and personal growth. This chapter explores the significance of positive distractions and offers guidance on how to incorporate them into your life.

Positive distractions serve as a respite from the thoughts and emotions associated with the detachment process. They provide an opportunity to immerse yourself in activities that bring you joy, fulfillment, and a sense of purpose.

Here are some examples of how you can practice positive distractions:
- Immersive Books and Movies: Engage in reading books or watching movies that captivate your attention and transport you to different worlds. Choose genres that resonate with you, whether it's fiction, non-fiction, fantasy, or self-help. Dive into captivating stories that allow you to temporarily escape and stimulate your imagination.
- Engaging Hobbies: Explore hobbies that you are passionate about or have always wanted to try. It could be painting, playing a musical instrument, cooking, gardening, or any other creative pursuit that brings you a sense of fulfillment and enjoyment. Dedicate time to immerse yourself in these activities and let your mind be absorbed by the process.
- Active Pursuits: Engage in physical activities or sports that require your focus and energy. It could be hiking, dancing, yoga, swimming, or any form of exercise that gets you moving and helps release endorphins. Physical activities not only distract your mind but also contribute to your overall well-being and boost your mood.

XXIX

engage in journaling prompts

Use journaling prompts to delve deeper into your thoughts and emotions. Reflect on questions such as "What does detaching mean to me?" or "How can I redefine my identity outside of this relationship?"

Journaling can be a powerful tool for self-reflection and introspection. When it comes to detachment and personal growth, engaging in journaling prompts can help you delve deeper into your thoughts, emotions, and experiences. This chapter explores the significance of journaling prompts and provides guidance on how to incorporate them into your practice.

Journaling prompts serve as catalysts for self-exploration and can help you gain clarity and insight into your detachment journey. By reflecting on specific questions or prompts, you open up a space for deeper understanding and introspection. Questions like "What does detaching mean to me?" or "How can I redefine my identity outside of this relationship?" prompt you to explore your beliefs, values, and aspirations. Journaling allows you to freely express your thoughts and emotions, helping you gain perspective and make meaning of your experiences.

Here are some examples of how to engage in journaling prompts:
- Set aside dedicated time for journaling: Establish a regular practice of journaling by setting aside a specific time each day or week. Find a quiet and comfortable space where you can focus and reflect without distractions.
- Choose journaling prompts that resonate with you: Select prompts that align with your personal journey of detachment and growth. You can find prompts in books, online resources, or even create your own based on the areas you wish to explore.
- Write freely and without judgment: When journaling, allow your thoughts to flow freely onto the pages without censoring or judging yourself. Embrace vulnerability and authenticity in your writing, knowing that it is a safe space for self-expression.

XXX

practice forgiveness exercises

Explore forgiveness practices that resonate with you, such as writing a forgiveness letter (even if you don't send it), practicing forgiveness meditation, or engaging in forgiveness rituals.

Forgiveness is a profound act of self-liberation and emotional healing. Engaging in forgiveness exercises allows us to let go of resentment, anger, and pain, and move towards greater inner peace and freedom. By exploring various forgiveness practices, we open ourselves up to the transformative power of forgiveness and create space for healing and growth.

One effective forgiveness exercise is writing a forgiveness letter. This practice involves expressing your thoughts, emotions, and reflections on the situation or person you're seeking forgiveness from. The letter serves as a cathartic release and an opportunity to process your feelings. Even if you choose not to send the letter, the act of writing can be therapeutic and help you release emotional attachments.

Engaging in forgiveness rituals is another way to practice forgiveness. These rituals can be personal and symbolic, tailored to your beliefs and preferences. For example, you may choose to light a candle, perform a release ceremony, or create an art piece that symbolizes forgiveness. The act of engaging in a forgiveness ritual serves as a tangible expression of your intention to let go and move forward.

Examples of forgiveness exercises:
- Write a forgiveness letter: Reflect on the situation or person you're seeking forgiveness from and write a heartfelt letter, expressing your emotions and intentions.
- Practice forgiveness meditation: Find a quiet space, close your eyes, and focus on your breath. Repeat forgiveness affirmations or phrases to cultivate forgiveness and compassion.
- Engage in forgiveness rituals: Create a personal ritual that symbolizes forgiveness, such as lighting a candle, performing a release ceremony, or creating art.

XXXI

engage in positive self-talk

Be mindful of the way you talk to yourself. Replace self-critical or negative thoughts with positive and affirming statements. Practice self-encouragement and remind yourself of your worth and strengths.

Engaging in positive self-talk becomes a powerful tool for nurturing self-esteem, resilience, and well-being. Our inner dialogue plays a significant role in shaping our perceptions of ourselves and the world around us. By consciously cultivating positive self-talk, we can reframe our thoughts, boost self-confidence, and foster a compassionate and empowering relationship with ourselves.

Being mindful of our self-talk involves paying attention to the way we speak to ourselves and challenging negative or self-critical thoughts. It requires developing awareness of our internal narratives and actively replacing them with positive and affirming statements. By consciously choosing supportive and empowering words, we can shift our mindset, cultivate self-compassion, and foster a belief in our worth and capabilities.

Examples of engaging in positive self-talk:
- Identify and challenge negative self-talk by questioning its validity and replacing it with positive affirmations.
- Practice self-encouragement by acknowledging your efforts, progress, and achievements, no matter how small.
- Use affirmations or positive statements to remind yourself of your strengths, resilience, and inherent worth.
- Surround yourself with supportive and uplifting influences, such as reading inspirational books or listening to motivating podcasts.
- Cultivate gratitude by focusing on the positive aspects of your life and expressing appreciation for yourself and others.

XXXII

seek inspiration from others

Read books, listen to podcasts, or watch videos of individuals who have gone through similar experiences and successfully detached from unhealthy relationships. Their stories can provide inspiration and guidance.

By actively seeking inspiration from others who have gone through similar experiences, we open ourselves up to new perspectives, tools, and strategies for detachment. Their stories can ignite our motivation, validate our emotions, and provide guidance as we navigate the challenging journey of letting go and moving forward.

Examples of how to practice seeking inspiration from others:
- Read "The Untethered Soul" by Michael A. Singer, which explores the process of detachment and inner freedom.
- Listen to podcasts such as "The Life Coach School Podcast" by Brooke Castillo or "The Overwhelmed Brain" by Paul Colaianni, which offer insights on detachment and personal growth.
- Watch TED Talks like "The Power of Vulnerability" by Brené Brown or "The Surprising Science of Happiness" by Dan Gilbert, which touch on themes of detachment, resilience, and finding joy.

XXXIII

seek support from a support network

Create a support system: Surround yourself with a strong support network of friends, family, or support groups. Share your experiences, seek guidance, and lean on others for support during challenging times.

Creating a support system is a vital component of the detachment process. Surrounding yourself with a strong network of friends, family, or support groups can provide invaluable guidance, understanding, and encouragement as you navigate the challenges of detachment. Sharing your experiences and leaning on others for support can offer comfort, validation, and a sense of belonging during this transformative journey.

Seek out individuals who are empathetic, non-judgmental, and supportive. Share your thoughts, emotions, and concerns with them, knowing that they will offer a listening ear and valuable insights. Engage in open and honest conversations, allowing yourself to be vulnerable and receive the support you need.

Examples of how to create a support system:
- Reach out to close friends or family members who have shown understanding and compassion in the past.
- Join a support group or seek therapy where you can connect with others who are going through similar experiences.
- Participate in online communities or forums focused on detachment, healing, and personal growth.
- Attend workshops, retreats, or seminars that provide a safe space for sharing and learning from others.
- Cultivate new friendships or rekindle existing connections with individuals who uplift and support you.

XXXIV

seek out nature

Spend time in nature to rejuvenate and reconnect with the world around you. Engaging in activities such as hiking, gardening, or simply taking a walk in a park can provide solace and perspective.

Nature has a remarkable way of soothing our souls and offering solace amidst life's challenges. In the process of detachment and personal growth, seeking out nature can be a powerful tool for rejuvenation and reconnecting with the world around us. This chapter explores the significance of spending time in nature and offers guidance on how to incorporate it into your life.

Nature has a unique ability to calm our minds and provide a sense of peace. Engaging in activities such as hiking, gardening, or simply taking a walk in a park allows us to immerse ourselves in the beauty and serenity of the natural world. The sights, sounds, and smells of nature awaken our senses and help us shift our focus away from our worries and concerns. Being in nature provides an opportunity for reflection, introspection, and gaining perspective on our lives.

Here are some examples of how to practice seeking out nature:
- Take regular nature walks: Set aside time each week to go for a walk in a nearby park, forest, or beach. Allow yourself to be fully present in the natural surroundings, taking in the sights, sounds, and sensations of the environment.
- Engage in outdoor activities: Explore outdoor activities that align with your interests, such as hiking, camping, kayaking, or birdwatching. These activities not only allow you to connect with nature but also provide a sense of adventure and exploration.
- Create a nature-inspired space: If access to nature is limited, create a small nature-inspired space in your home or office. Bring in plants, natural elements like rocks or shells, and incorporate natural light and sounds to create a peaceful and calming atmosphere.

XXXV

seek professional help if needed

If you find it challenging to detach or if the emotions become overwhelming, consider reaching out to a therapist or counselor. They can provide guidance, support, and specialized techniques to help you navigate the process.

Seeking professional help is an important option to consider if you find it challenging to detach from someone or if the emotions become overwhelming. Therapists and counselors are trained professionals who can provide guidance, support, and specialized techniques to help you navigate the detachment process in a healthy and empowering way. They offer a safe and non-judgmental space where you can explore your feelings, gain insights, and develop coping strategies tailored to your unique needs.

A therapist or counselor can assist you in various ways during the detachment process. They can help you understand and process your emotions, gain perspective on the relationship dynamics, and explore any underlying issues that may be contributing to your attachment. They can also provide you with tools and techniques to manage your emotions, set boundaries, and cultivate self-care practices. Ultimately, seeking professional help can be a valuable investment in your emotional well-being and personal growth.

Examples of how to practice seeking professional help:
- Research and find a therapist or counselor who specializes in relationships, emotional well-being, or detachment.
- Schedule an initial consultation to discuss your situation and assess whether the therapist is a good fit for your needs.
- Engage in regular therapy sessions to explore your feelings, gain insights, and develop strategies for detachment.
- Be open and honest with your therapist, sharing your experiences, challenges, and goals.
- Collaborate with your therapist to develop a personalized plan that aligns with your needs and objectives.

XXXVI

embrace solitude

Take time for yourself to reflect, recharge, and reconnect with your inner self. Solitude can provide an opportunity for introspection and self-discovery.

Embracing solitude is a valuable aspect of the detachment process. This chapter explores the importance of taking time for oneself, away from distractions and external influences, in order to reflect, recharge, and reconnect with one's inner self. Solitude provides a space for introspection, self-discovery, and personal growth, allowing individuals to gain clarity and find inner peace.

In our fast-paced and connected world, solitude often gets overlooked or misunderstood. However, spending time alone is not a sign of loneliness or isolation but rather an intentional choice to nurture one's well-being and deepen the detachment journey. Embracing solitude allows individuals to tune into their inner thoughts, emotions, and desires without external distractions, enabling them to develop a deeper understanding of themselves and their needs.

Here are some examples of how to practice embracing solitude:
- Carve out quiet time: Set aside regular periods of time where you can be alone with your thoughts and feelings. Find a quiet and comfortable space where you can reflect, meditate, or simply be present in the moment.
- Engage in solo activities: Discover activities that you enjoy doing alone, such as taking walks in nature, journaling, painting, or reading. These activities can provide a sense of peace and rejuvenation, allowing you to reconnect with yourself on a deeper level.
- Practice mindfulness: Incorporate mindfulness into your daily routine. Pay attention to your thoughts, emotions, and sensations in the present moment without judgment. This practice enhances self-awareness and helps cultivate a sense of inner calm.

XXXVII

focus on personal growth

Use the opportunity of detachment to invest in your personal growth and development. Engage in activities that help you discover new aspects of yourself, develop new skills, and build a stronger sense of self.

Detaching from someone can provide a unique opportunity for personal growth and development. By shifting your focus towards your own growth, you can use the energy and time that was once invested in the relationship to invest in yourself. Engaging in activities that facilitate self-discovery, skill development, and self-improvement can help you build resilience, confidence, and a stronger sense of self.

Take this time to explore new interests, hobbies, or passions that have always intrigued you. Engage in activities that bring you joy, challenge you, and help you uncover new aspects of yourself. Whether it's learning a musical instrument, taking up painting, or trying out a new sport, embracing new experiences can foster personal growth and broaden your horizons.

Examples of how to focus on personal growth:
- Set personal goals that align with your values and aspirations, and work towards achieving them.
- Enroll in courses or workshops that allow you to learn new skills or deepen your knowledge in areas of interest.
- Engage in self-reflection and journaling to gain insights into your strengths, weaknesses, and areas for personal growth.
- Seek out mentors or role models who can provide guidance and support in your personal development journey.
- Prioritize self-care by engaging in activities that promote physical, emotional, and mental well-being.
- Surround yourself with inspiring and supportive individuals who encourage your personal growth.

XXXVIII

reflect on your progress

Take time to reflect on how far you've come in your detachment journey. Celebrate the milestones and small victories along the way, and acknowledge the growth and resilience you have demonstrated.

In the process of detaching from someone and moving forward, it's important to take moments to reflect on your progress. This chapter explores the significance of self-reflection and celebrating your achievements. By acknowledging how far you've come, you can gain perspective, boost your self-confidence, and stay motivated on your journey of detachment.

Reflecting on your progress allows you to appreciate the milestones and small victories you've achieved. It serves as a reminder of your growth, resilience, and the positive changes you've made. By consciously acknowledging and celebrating your achievements, you reinforce a sense of empowerment and build momentum to continue moving forward.

Here are some examples of how to practice reflecting on your progress:
- Set aside dedicated time for self-reflection. Find a quiet and comfortable space where you can focus without distractions.
- Journal about your journey. Write about the challenges you've faced, the lessons you've learned, and the progress you've made. Acknowledge the positive changes you've noticed in yourself and the actions you've taken towards detachment.
- Create a "Progress Jar." Fill a jar with notes or small items that represent your milestones and achievements. Whenever you accomplish something significant or experience a positive breakthrough, write it down or add an item to the jar. Take moments to review the contents of the jar and appreciate how far you've come.

XXXIX

celebrate your progress

Acknowledge and celebrate the progress you've made in detaching from the person. Recognize each step forward, no matter how small, and give yourself credit for your resilience and growth.

It is essential to recognize and celebrate the progress you have made along the way. Each step forward, no matter how small, is a testament to your strength, resilience, and commitment to personal growth. This chapter delves into the importance of acknowledging your achievements and provides guidance on how to celebrate your progress throughout the detachment journey.

Celebrating progress begins with cultivating self-awareness and mindfulness. Take moments of reflection to acknowledge the milestones you have reached and the positive changes you have experienced. Recognize the strength and courage it took to let go and create healthier boundaries.

Here are some examples of how to celebrate progress:
- Create a Progress Journal: Keep a journal dedicated to documenting your journey of detachment. Write down the challenges you have overcome, the lessons you have learned, and the growth you have experienced. Revisit this journal regularly to remind yourself of how far you have come.
- Treat Yourself: Reward yourself for the progress you have made. It could be as simple as indulging in your favorite treat, pampering yourself with a spa day, or taking a day off to engage in activities that bring you joy. Allow yourself to savor and enjoy these moments of self-appreciation.
- Share with Others: Celebrate your progress by sharing your achievements with trusted friends or family members who have supported you throughout the detachment process. Their encouragement and recognition can amplify your sense of accomplishment and reinforce the positive changes you have made.

thank you

Your commitment to your well-being and personal growth is truly inspiring, and we are honored to have been a part of your process.

Thank you for choosing "How do I Detach from Someone? A Guide to Detaching and Rediscovering Yourself" as your companion on this journey of growth and healing. May the lessons learned and the practices shared continue to serve as a source of empowerment, guiding you towards a future filled with self-love, joy, and limitless possibilities.

Lucy Monday
www.forever-winter.com

Printed in Great Britain
by Amazon